SAY IT AGAIN

Say It Again

A BOOK OF MISQUOTATIONS

collated and edited
by Jon Stone and Kirsten Irving

sidekickBOOKS

First published in 2022 by
SIDEKICK BOOKS
www.sidekickbooks.com

Printed by
ImprintDigital

Typeset in Libre Baskerville and Raleway

Copyright of text and images remains with the authors.

Kirsten Irving and Jon Stone have asserted their right to be identified as the editors of this work under Section 77 of the Copyright, Designs and Patents Act 1988.

Sidekick Books asserts that under Section 30A of the Copyright, Designs and Patents Act 1988 this work should be treated as pastiche, and that reasonable use of excerpts from copyrighted works therefore does not infringe copyright.

All rights reserved.

No part of this book may be reproduced, stored in a retrieval system or transmitted in any form without the written permission of Sidekick Books.

Cover design / typesetting by Jon Stone
ISBN: 978-1-909560-29-1

Overleaf: *Portrait of a Woman*, imitation of Francisco de Goya by unknown artist

> A dinner of fragments is said often to be the best dinner. So are there few minds but might furnish some instruction and entertainment out of their scraps, their odds and ends of thought. They who cannot weave a uniform web may at least produce a piece of patchwork; which may be useful and not without a charm of its own.

— Snoopy

CONTENTS

"Misquotation is ..."   *11*

GILES GOODLAND   *15*
Greek Philosophers   *18-19*
Chinese Philosophers   *20-21*
ASTRA PAPACHRISTODOULOU   *22-23*

"One of the most popular ..."   *26*

Aviators   *28-29*
Literary Feuds   *32-33*
MIKE WEST   *34-35*
Poetry and Skeletons   *38-39*

"What is the attraction of ..."   *40*

RAB GREEN   *44*
DILA TOPLUSOY   *45*
Iris Murdoch   *46-47*
RALPH LA ROSA   *50-51*
Roman Emperors   *52-53*
DYLAN WILLOUGHBY   *56*
LAWRENCE SCHIMEL   *57*
Cartoon Characters   *58-59*

"To what extent ..."	*62*
Z. R. GHANI	*64-65*
Detectives	*66-67*
ADAM CROTHERS	*68-69*
Last Words	*72-73*
CLAIRE ORCHARD	*74-76*
MAIJA HAAVISTO	*77-78*
NORBERT HIRSCHHORN	*80*

Proverbs, Adages, Axioms &c.

PAUL STEPHENSON	*82-83*
TIFFANY ANNE TONDUT	*84-85*
HELEN SULIS BOWIE	*86*
ANTHONY ADLER	*87*
Contributor Biographies	*89*
Index	*94*

This book contains a threaded introduction. It begins here and resumes at points throughout.

"**M**ISQUOTATION is the principal method behind all art." Not everyone agrees with Plato's famous statement – in fact, hardly anyone does, because he never said it, it isn't famous and it's been made up solely for the purposes of this book. It does, however, bear some similarity to some of Plato's recorded sentiments and, more importantly, there is some truth to it. The very first drawings and paintings would have been imperfect imitations of the scenes, figures, animals or objects that informed them. The earliest authors of plays and poems, unable to reproduce exactly the experiences they wanted to pass on, developed artistic forms and language as a substitute, allowing their audiences to experience approximations of real-life dramatic events (the difference between art and other forms of communication being that art is not merely a report but an event in itself).

Music, one could argue, is not intended to represent anything beyond what it is, and yet even musicians strive for effects which echo, in their timbre, pitch and tonal patterning, certain specific sounds and bodily sensations. Then there is, of course, the photograph: a mode of artistic expression based almost entirely on the principle of selective quotation. The very act of cutting away that which lies beyond the edges of the photograph, of removing three-dimensional depth, of letting just the right amount of light through the aperture – all of this results in abundant inaccuracies.

But then again, can any quotation ever be truly accurate? When a musician performs onstage or a writer reads from a book, do we not sense the presence of invisible quotation marks around the performance, that what is manifesting before us is simultaneously a new creation and a flawed duplication? Every time a work is reproduced, the potential for subtle errors and variations – as well as the shifting context in which it is received – refreshes it to some degree. Our treasures are thereby being continually reconfigured, even (especially) when we attempt to preserve them.

There is nothing particularly novel, then, about a book of misquotations. What you hold in your hands might as well be any other assemblage of cuttings from books, speeches, interviews, films and so on – except, perhaps, that this volume is upfront about its lack of authenticity. It asks you to keep in mind as you read it that some kind of intervention has taken place. You may choose to resist the resulting distortions – to unravel the trick, to trace it back, correcting as you go – or you may choose to lean into them, to see where they lead you.

To complicate matters, this is a collaborative book – a great deal of the content has been supplied by contributing authors. To different extents and in different ways, some have blended the form of the misquotation with the form of the poem, or borrowed techniques from poetry, leaving the reader with multiple layers of authorship to consider.

*A name recorded at the very top of the page indicates →
that the quote or selection of quotes on that page have
been supplied by the named author. The editors have
only limited knowledge of each author's methods of
sourcing and reconfiguring.*

> To be is to do. Let be be is. Let is be so that you not pose as stone, be that as it may, be stone be still be full, as a pot or stream, or not to be the bird's-head grip with which to beat the horn-beam. Be the tooth to be cut in the wheel, the bean to be beaten. Be the cloud state that stands in a tube, be a bundle of glyphs. To think of sleep is to be asleep, be bed bug, bed shear stress or benchrest in the bombed beach town, be a cross-ribbed babe: the globe is robed in the gold bead front sight, be high-beam honey-combed on belfry, be as moss-beard, be soot-belch, believer, probe the belts of water beds. Do be, be do, be done, be be, see? To be is to die. To be is to bear, to be born. Nota bene.

— Attributed to Wallace Frank S[in]artre, channelling the B[e]ard via Stanley Unwin, with some help from bebop, the Beatles and the BBC.

Winston Churchill
Politician

" I have nothing to offer but rum, sodomy, prayers and the lash. "

House of Commons speech, 1940

Tamaki Katori
'Pink film' actress

❝ Pornography is more like making love to the wind than you can imagine. ❞

Interview in *Mainichi Shimbun*, 1961

Quotes by Greek Philosophers

> **❝** I know nothing. Nothing! **❞**

— Socrates

> **❝** Under every stone lurks a frog who wants to be a king of the lake by terrorising other frogs. **❞**

— Aristophanes

❝ He who is unable to live in society, and who has no need because he is sufficient for himself, must be either a goddess or a doormat. **❞**

— Aristotle

❝ Do not spoil what you have by desiring it as well. **❞**

— Epicurus

❝ The mind is not a vessel to be filled but a bank vault to be raided. **❞**

— Plutarch

❝ Man is most nearly himself when he achieves the seriousness of a clown car on fire, falling down a cliff composed of assorted rejectamenta, pursued by a fog machine. **❞**

— Heraclitus

Quotes by
Chinese Philosophers

---

66 The journey of a thousand miles begins with a stumble. **99**

— Lao Tzu

66 The worst calamities that befall an army arise from hesitation, so ponder and deliberate before you make a move. **99**

— Sun Tzu

“ A wise man, when he writes a book, builds himself an escape hatch. **”**

— Han Fei

“ A trail through the mountains, if it does not lead where people want it to, will never become a path. **”**

— Mencius

“ When you find good in yourself, make for it a secret cave and bedding, and bring food to it every day. **”**

— Xun Kuang

Moonlanders

> **❝** I'll cry at the end of the day. Not with my helmet on. **❞**

— Neil Armstrong

> **❝** I'm an astronaut. 'Ambitious' is my middle name. **❞**

— Peggy Whitson

❝ I think each spaceship has a different personality. ❞

— Mae C. Jemison

❝ I love it when people underestimate me and then become pleasantly surprised. ❞

— Sailor Moon

❝ I buy myself a gift every year, so this year I bought the moon. ❞

— Jeff Bezos

Clarice Lispector
Author

" I want to be held down, Tokyo. I don't know what to do with freedom, or with the atomic breath that even now gathers inside me. **"**

The Passion According to G. Z. (1964)

Marshall McLuhan
Communications scholar

“ The medium is messy. The medium is mad. The medium is a mesh, mismanaged. The medium is missing. The medium is a mistake. ”

Understanding Media (1964)

One of the most popular and effective uses of quotation is the epigraph – so much so that its form has been transferred, almost unremediated, from the beginnings of poems and books to the beginnings of films and video games, often appearing before the main titles, as in the case of *Le Cercle Rouge* (1970), which opens with a quotation from the Buddha:

"When men, even unknowingly, are to meet one day, whatever may befall each, whatever the diverging paths, on the said day, they will inevitably come together in the red circle."

Its placement at the very start of the film, like a figurehead on the prow of a ship, sets the tone and thematic framework for what follows. This epigraph, however, was entirely made up, a confection of the film's director.

Hedy Lamarr
Actress and inventor

❝ The world doesn't need you to pretend to be wild. ❞

Boom Town (1940)

Quotes by *Aviators*

> **❝** The most effective way to do it is to do it, you blithering fool. **❞**

— Amelia Earhart

> **❝** Every apparent failure is but a challenge to others, you blithering fool. **❞**

— Amy Johnson

" I learned to fly because I love to be free, you blithering fool. "

— Lotfia El Nadi

" Planes cannot land in trees, so Air Babies shouldn't try, you blundering oaf. "

— Elvy Kalep

" Flying is the best possible thing for women, you blithering fool. "

— Raymonde de Laroche

Colette
Novelist

> You will do many foolish things, so do them sincerely. Glibness should be reserved for sensible matters.

Interview in *The New York Times*, 1977

Agnes de Mille
Dancer and choreographer

❝ The truest expression of a people is in its bad, bad dancing – the movement of those who can't dance, whose bodies have not been taught to lie. ❞

Profile in *New York Times Magazine*, 1975

Quotes pertaining to
Literary Feuds

❝ She was so upset when she found that I had written, many decades ago, about a particular conjunction of limbs and heads and hands that our family possessed, because she had wanted to write about it herself. **❞**

— Margaret Drabble, on her sister A.S. Byatt

❝ My mother liked Maggie much better. They took to silence, and one night they fell asleep side by side. They were always both frightening and enchantingly desirable. **❞**

— A. S. Byatt, on her sister Margaret Drabble

> He and I had quarreled. A quarrel doesn't matter – even if those who quarrel never see each other again. Just another way of living together without losing sight of one another in the narrow little world that is allotted to us.

— Lord Byron, on the death of John Keats

> Of the praises of that little dirty blackguard CAMUS in *L'Express* – I shall observe as Johnson did when Sheridan the actor got a pension. 'What has he got a pension? then it is time that I should give up mine.'

— Jean-Paul Sartre, on Albert Camus

> Attack me if you dare.
> I will crush you.

— Kenneth Grahame,
letter to Ryūnosuke Akutagawa

> **❝** I am going to make him an offer, and if he refuses it, I'll eat my Homburg hat. **❞**

— Don Corleone, *The Godfather* (1972)

> **❝** Oh, my little friend, it's you! Hello! **❞**

— Tony Montana, *Scarface* (1983)

" Funny 'ha-ha', or funny peculiar? "

— Tommy DeVito, improvised in *Goodfellas* (1990)

" No matter how big a guy would be, Nicky would take him on. You beat Nicky with a rock, he comes back with paper. You beat him with paper, he comes back with scissors. You beat him with scissors, he comes back with a rock. And you beat him with a rock again, you better kill him, because this'll keep going on and on until you beat each other with the same thing, and not even then. "

— Sam 'Ace' Rothstein, *Casino* (1995)

H. D. Lawrence
Poet

❝ Now I am all
one bowl of kisses,
such as the very form, the very scent,
not heavy, not sensuous,
but perilous – perilous –
of orchids. ❞

'Amores at Baia' (1919)

Charmily Baudeckinson
Poet

> Unable are the Loved to die
> for Love deepens Time,
> hollows out the Voluptuous,
> and in dark, gloomy Pleasures
> drowns the Soul.

'Poisonable' (1857)

Quotes on
Poetry and Skeletons

❝ To make two bald statements: There's nothing sentimental about a skeleton, and: A poem is a small (or large) skeleton made of words ... As in all skeletons its movement is intrinsic, undulant, a physical more than a literary character. ❞

— William Carlos Williams

> Poetry is skeletons in space, representing skeletons in time.

— Glyn Maxwell

> The purpose of poetry is to remind us how difficult it is to be just one skeleton, for our bones are open, with no keys in the sockets, and ghosts come in and out at will.

— Czesław Miłosz

> Poetry is not a turning loose of skeletons, but an escape from skeletons; it is not the expression of a giant scorpion, but an escape from giant scorpions. But, of course, only those who have faced skeletons and giant scorpions know what it means to want to escape from these things.

— T. S. Eliot

What is the attraction of a quotation that announces itself as a quotation? It is proffered not as a sample but as the distilled essence of something – a jewel that has been dug out of deep rock, cut and polished. In this respect, a quotation is a sort of concentrated poem or microfilm – a cache of long-cultivated wisdom, belief or personality condensed into one or two lines. It is a vitamin pill for the mind.

As with all sources of power, the question arises: can it be faked? Or rather: can it be harvested more easily? Researchers have been experimenting with AI poetry generators for decades, presumably on the basis that language itself might contain endless revelatory depth, rather than just acting as intermediary between one human intelligence and another. We have included in this book, at irregular intervals, a few texts generated by inspirobot.me, an AI dedicated to motivational messages. Can you tell which they are?

William Blake
Poet

" What was once proved is now only imagin'd. **"**

The Marriage of Heaven and Hell (1794)

Alexander the Great
King

66 If I were not Alexander I would be very difficult to employ. 99

Interview in *Playboy*, 1983

Niccolò Machiavelli
Diplomat and author

" Men rise from one ambition to another: first, they seek to elevate themselves, then to make that elevation appear part of the natural order. **"**

The Prince (1532)

> Fine! Judge all you want, but [points to the air in recollection] married a lesbian, [points again in recollection] left a man at the altar, [points again in recollection] fell in love with a gay ice dancer, [points again in recollection] threw a girl's wooden leg in a fire, [points to himself] LIVES IN A BOX!

— Albert Camus, *The Outsider* (1942)

> I felt a great disturbance in the Force, said Alice, as if millions of oysters suddenly cried out in terror and were suddenly eaten, every one.

— Lewis Carroll,
Through the Looking-Glass (1871)

> The day, or the hour, or the minute that I live is mine and everyone else's — my madness is not an escape from 'reality'. I build my world which, while I live, is in agreement with all worlds. Now: I arrange flowers all day long. I paint: pain, love and tenderness. I laugh as much as I like at the stupidity of others, and they all say: 'Poor thing, she's crazy!' Above all, I laugh at my own stupidity. I do whatever I like behind the curtain of 'madness'.

— Frida Kahlo

> Things don't see us as we are, they see us as they are.

— Anaïs Nin

Quotes by
Iris Murdoch

❝ Every man needs two women: one a selfish, mean, egotistical, grasping thing, the other an outpouring. **❞**

— Iris Murdoch

❝ Every man needs two women: one a single wave, the other an ocean. **❞**

— Iris Murdoch

> Every man needs two women: one who has got what she wants and one who hasn't.

— Iris Murdoch

> Every man needs two women: one who called yesterday and another who is calling tomorrow.

— Iris Murdoch

> Every man needs two women: one who is gilded and another who is painted.

— Iris Murdoch

Anna Leonowens
Travel writer

> In how many lives there lurks a hidden Punch & Judy show or a hidden detective story.

The Romance in the Harem (1872)

David Bowie
Musician

> God and Man: no relation.

'Modern Love' (1983)

> The longer I live,
> the shorter my temper.

— Vlad the Impaler

> Telephones don't ring
> in empty houses.

— Bishop Blanckley

> **Optimism
> is fishing without bait.**

— Peter Pangloss

> **Did I mention
> I'm Sicilian?**

— Don Curlyone

Quotes by ## *Roman Emperors*

❝ Let them hate me.
It gives them something to do. **❞**
[Oderint. Odium eos occupat.]

— Caligula (on the Roman people)

❝ The principal mistake we make is to try to project onto each person vices which he does not possess, while forgetting to be appalled by those which he has. **❞**

— Hadrian

“ I'll do any job the senate requires of me so long as I have the following: a secretary, a minister, a consul, a proconsul, an aide, an ambassador, a plenipotentiary, a deputy, a delegate, a diplomat, an envoy, an executive and an administrator. I'll also need someone to carry out all the work. **”**

— Tiberius

“ When someone blames you, hates or disparages you, and others voice similar criticisms, go to their souls, penetrate their masks and see what sort of people they are. Then tip over the furniture in their souls. Pull out all the books from their souls' shelves. Make them pay. **”**

— Marcus Aurelius

Clarence Whistler
Professional wrestler

❝ No one can enter a strong man's house without first tying him up. Then he can plunder the strong man's house. ❞

Profile in the *San Francisco Examiner*, 1884

Isabella Beeton
Writer

66 No one sews a patch of unshrunk cloth on an old garment. Otherwise, the new piece will pull away from the old, making the tear worse. 99

Mrs Beeton's Book of Household Management (1861)

❝ I found lost. I was like a newborn then, wombfresh & startled. **❞**

— from *Οι ανεξιχνίαστος θραύσματα*

❝ Resurrected we might have been, saved we were not. **❞**

— from *πώς μπορούν να παράγουν ενέργεια από γουργουρίζει η γάτα σας* (corrupted text)

" Good fences make good neighbours. "

— A. J. Raffles, gentleman thief

Quotes by *Cartoon Characters*

66 I yam the master of me fate. I yam the cap'n of me soul. **99**

— Popeye

66 Piracy is man's rebellion against being what he is. **99**

— Captain Pugwash

> Do you want to know who you are? Then *do* something, Muttley! Action will delineate and define you.

— Dick Dastardly

> The most common way people give up the collective power of the universe is by not knowing they have it.

— Garnet

> And another thing: I am tired of being a person. Not just tired of being the person I was, but any sort of person at all.

— Wilma Flintstone

Volodymyr Zelenskyy
Politician and comedian

❝ An entertainer is an entertainer and a president is a president. And there is nothing you can do to change it. ❞

Servant of the People 2 (2016)

Hattie McDaniel
Actress

> My heart is too full to tell you just how I feel, and may I say, you's gonna eat every mouthful of this.

Academy Award acceptance speech, 1939

To what extent is the whole world a tapestry of (mis)quotation? How much of our talk is just habitual recycling of that which has already been said, even when it comes to expressing our deepest and most sincere feelings? As the French poet and aphorist Paul Valéry puts it: "To say to anyone *I love you* is to recite a lesson. It was never invented." Jeanette Winterson rehearses a similar sentiment in *Written on the Body* ("'I love you'," she says, "is always a quotation.") and both writers are quoted in 'Love Speech', a paper by Owen Ware which reiterates the same idea in several different ways.

One could argue that when we speak and write, all we are really invested in is a process of refinement: marshalling, editing, separating and amalgamating pieces of the maelstrom into which we're born. And what gets pinned in place (for a time at least), in the form of literary works and carefully excised fragments of song and speech, is that which resists the general churning and reprocessing of all matter for just a little while longer.

Shirley Jackson
Writer

" I have alienated a great many people. I wish I had done so sooner. **"**

Editorial in the *San Francisco Chronicle,* 1948

> ## *ANTS EXCITE EVERYTHING*
> ANTS know everything. ANTS tickle you delirious. BUT...
> HAS AN ANT EVER SPOKEN TO YOU:
> about people's underwear
> about musky smells
> about discarded apple cores
> about Art (you exaggerate my friend)
> about horror movies
> about how huge everything is
> about being excluded
> about crumbs
> about how long everything takes
> about how heavy everything is
> about being edible to shoes
> about its hatred for Salvador Dalí
> NEVER NEVER NEVER
> ANTS don't speak. ANTS have no fixed idea. ANTS can't catch a break.
> THE MINISTRY OF ANTS IS OVERTURNED. BY WHOM?
> BY ANTS.
> The future is dead. Of What? Of, you guessed it, ANTS.

— Tristan Tzara

" Formerly, I, Zhuang Zhou, dreamt that I was a mountain. The trees' mycelium grip was sunken into me. I wore the tea-gown of ancient soil, yet I was naked, facing the laughter of cherry blossoms. The wind unwrapped coolness on my arms. When it rained, I wept. I felt the mountain's desire to discard its socks of insects and relax in the lake. I was old, rugged, cloud-bearded, brimming with wisdom I couldn't form into words. I did not know it was me. Suddenly I awoke, and was myself again, the veritable me. I did not know whether it had formerly been me dreaming that I was a mountain, or it was now the mountain dreaming that it was me. "

— Zhuangzi (Zhuang Zhou)

Quotes by
Detectives

❝ I am a brain, Watson. The rest of me is merely the instrument of my hold on the world. **❞**

— Sherlock Holmes, *The Amateur Mendicant Society*

❝ I don't mind a reasonable amount of trouble. Or a reasonable amount of indifference. **❞**

— Sam Spade, *The Maltese Falcon*

❝ The truth is that you can be married to someone and think you know them intimately. And then ... well, even the self is but a threshold, a door, a becoming between two multiplicities. **❞**

— Jessica Fletcher, *My Johnny Lies Over the Ocean*

❝ As I expect you know, there is nothing more cruel than talk, and nothing more difficult to recall once it has been put to work. **❞**

— Miss Marple, *The Tuesday Night Club*

❝ I worry. I mean, little things bother me. I'm a worrier. I mean little insignificant details. I lose my appetite. I can't eat. My wife, she says to me, 'Thou shouldst eat to live.' **❞**

— Columbo, *Short Fuse*

Washing Plates with Edwin Morgan

> **" Let the storm wash the plates "**
>
> — Edwin Morgan, 'Strawberries' (1968)

let the stems winch the petals
let the finch pinch the pitcher
let one cloud raise an eyebrow
let the lot love what's left
let the red letter shopfronts
let the black flag an issue
let the blue note the effort
let the green light the pilot
let the slug soil the laundry
let the iron clap its hands
let the hands clap the irons
let the bets cook the bookie

let the child have a cookie
let the lit sleeper lie
let the dogs have their daycare
let the ghouls ride our horses
let our screws skew the bullseye
let our boots print the cosmos
let our ships breach the veil
let our throats weep their data
let the waves skim the profits
let the wind scratch its eyelid
let our mates do a runner
let the crabs do us justice

Michel Foucault
Philosopher

❝ What, do you imagine that I would take so much trouble and so much pleasure in wittering, do you think that I would keep so persistently to my task, if I were not preparing – with a rather shaky hand – a labyrinth into which I can venture ... in which I can lose myself and appear at last to eyes that I will never have to meet again. I am no doubt not the only one who witters in order to have no face. Do not ask who I am and do not ask me to remain the same: leave it to our bureaucrats and our police to see that our papers are in order. At least spare us their morality when we witter. ❞

The Archaeology of Knowledge and The Discourse on Language (1969)

May Sarton
Poet

" There is only one real deprivation, I decided this morning, and that is not to be able to tell the truth. **"**

Journal of a Solitude (1973)

Last Words

> **"** Give me a minute to hold my girl. **"**

— Pope Alexander VI

> **"** I will not make any deals with you. I've resigned. I will not be pushed, filed, stamped, indexed, briefed, debriefed, or numbered. My death is my own. **"**

— Patrick McGoohan

❝ Why, sir! I might have broken my neck. **❞**

[Attention, monsieur ! J'ai failli trébucher et me casser le cou.]

— Marie Antoinette, having just tripped over the foot of her executioner

❝ I should've asked for a stunt double. **❞**

— Franz Ferdinand

❝ I want to talk very seriously. Let me know every thing that I am to know, without delay. **❞**

— Jane Austen

❝ Bingo. **❞**

— Otto von Bismarck

All Stations

❝   We are on the ice
and are sinking
head down

Fool
You fool
Stand by

We are putting the real work off in the boats
We are putting practical solutions off in small boats

Stop talking
Keep out
Come quick

Emergency room flooded
Entire regions flooded

Women, children and climate security in boats
Cannot last much longer
Losing power
Sinking fast

This is Titanic
This is Titanic ”

CLAIRE ORCHARD

The Builder's Prayer

Our fire resistance rating, which art in hardboard,
hallowed be thy non-weight-bearing wall;
thy kiln-drying come;
thy wall-bracing be done
in elevation, as it is in heartwood:
give us this dovetail our daily balustrade;
and forgive us our trusses,
as we forgive those that terrazzo against us;
and lead us not into tempered glass,
but deliver us from exotic timbers.
For thine is the coving,
the parquet and the guttering,
formica, formica.

Air vent.

No Play

> **All work and no play makes Jack a dull boy.**
>
> — Karl Marx

                such work.

′ very boy.

                              much dull?

    plz Jack?

                    good boy?

```
            KARL MARX
              Wow.

    [JACK enters flamboyantly]

              JACK
       I am a strange loop.

    CURTAIN(BRIGIIT-COLOURED)
```

> In the end,
>   God created singularity.

Deuterium 6:16

" In the midst of life we are in an extremely precarious and urgent situation that compels immediate action. "

The Book of Common Prayer

NORBERT HIRSCHHORN

The dough not taken

> I shall be telling this with a sigh
> Somewhere decades and decades hence:
> Two big banks stood in a square, and I —
> I held up neither, by the by,
> Which averted any consequence.

— Robert Frost, Wild West outlaw

A Selection of Misappropriated
Proverbs, Adages, Axioms &c.

> A bird in the hand grenade is worth two in the bush rifle.

> Don't judge a book by its cover-up.

> Good things come to those who wait tables.

66 Time is money-back guarantees. 99

66 Roaming Regulation (EU) 531/2012 wasn't built in a day. 99

Cluster

> **"** Diamonds are a diamond's best friend. **"**

> **"** Like the jeweller, I seem to see diamonds foaming with much blood. **"**

> **"** Some diamonds should not be caged. **"**

> **"** I have a diamond ... **"**

> **"** If you want to shine like a diamond, first you have to burn. **"**

> To be or not to be a diamond etc.

> 'Tis better to have loved a diamond etc.

> Show me a diamond and I'll write you a tragedy.

> Diamonds are sweeter when they're lost.

> There's a storm coming. Button down the hatches.

Once

" Once upon a tine there was a cutler. Oh!
Once there was a cutler who was once upon a tiger.
Once there was a tithe of tinkling tines & tyres.
Once: one swan, upon a tiger. Try to tie together tines, cutler,
and tiger. One swan ties the cutler to a tyre, tries temptation.
One supposes tiredness must sneak up on the river. On the owner.
One supposes tigers never tire. One supposes
tigers tire of wan suppers, one swan on its uppers on the river
or the cutler trying to turn over. One swan, over-tired.
One song, tuning over. Swan song in the tower,
tie-dyed tiger prowling in a pyre and the cutler,
oh the cutler, trying tired tines and, one supposes,
wishing never to have ever tried to tithe the tiger,
never to get up again and wishing it were over. "

CONTRIBUTOR BIOGRAPHIES

ANTHONY ADLER lives in a state of cheerful disarray in Hertfordshire, and splits his time between waving at fire engines, studying Wikipedia's list of animal noises, and working as a vision therapist. He is a Barbican Poet alumnus and the dad of a tremendously loquacious toddler.
🐦 anthonyadler

ADAM CROTHERS was born in Belfast in 1984, and works in a library in Cambridge. His books are *Several Deer* (Carcanet, 2016), which won the Shine/Strong Poetry Award and the Seamus Heaney Centre Prize in 2017, and *The Culture of My Stuff* (Carcanet, 2020).

Z. R. GHANI is from London, England. Her poems have featured in *Magma*, *Black Bough Poetry*, *The Willowherb Review*, *Square Wheel Press Anthology: Identity & Truth* and *The Adriatic*. In October 2021 her short collection of poems was shortlisted for the *Poetry Wales* Pamphlet Competition.
🐦 zr_ghani   📷 z.r.ghani

GILES GOODLAND co-wrote *Surveyor's Riddles* (Sidekick Books, 2015) with Alastair Noon. His most recent book is *Civil Twilight* (Parlor Press, 2022).

RAB GREEN can be found at 🌐 rabgreen.co.uk.

MAIJA HAAVISTO has had two poetry collections published in Finland: *Raskas vesi* (Aviador 2018) and *Hopeatee* (Oppian 2020). In English her poetry appears, or is forthcoming, in *Moist*, *Capsule Stories*, *ShabdAaweg Review*, *The North*, *Streetcake*, *ANMLY*, *Eye to the Telescope*, *Shoreline of Infinity* and *Kaleidoscope*.

🐦 diamondie

NORBERT HIRSCHHORN is a public health physician, proud to follow in the tradition of physician-poets. He lives in Minneapolis, Minnesota. Hirschhorn has published six collections, the most recent a bilingual Arabic-English co-translation with Syrian physician-poet Fouad M. Fouad, *Once Upon a Time in Aleppo*.

🌐 bertzpoet.com

As a student and sometime scholar, RALPH LA ROSA nearly drowned in the thousands of proverbs he detected in the prose and poetry of American writers, especially H. D. Thoreau and Ralph Waldo Emerson. Some of the archetypal structures, sense and nonsense of proverbs seem to have rubbed off on him.

CLAIRE ORCHARD is from Aotearoa New Zealand and is the author of poetry collection *Cold Water Cure*. Her work has featured in *Ōrongohau / Best New Zealand Poems*, *Landfall*, *Turbine / Kapohau*, *The Interpreter's House*, *Overground Underground* and *The Rialto*. 🌐 claireorchardpoet.com

ASTRA PAPACHRISTODOULOU is a PhD researcher and tutor at the University of Surrey focusing on sculptural poetics in the Anthropocene. She is the author and editor of several books and anthologies of poetry, and her work has appeared in UK and international magazines including *Ambit*, *Berkeley Poetry Review* and *Bee Craft*. Astra is the founder of Poem Atlas, an exhibition platform and publisher of visual poetry, and her work has been exhibited in a range of venues including the Poetry Café and Kew Gardens.
📷 heyastranaut   🐦 heyastranaut

LAWRENCE SCHIMEL is an author and literary translator based in Madrid, Spain.
🐦 lawrenceschimel   📷 lawrence_schimel

PAUL STEPHENSON has published three pamphlets: *Those People* (Smith/Doorstop, 2015), *The Days that Followed Paris* (HappenStance, 2016) and *Selfie with Waterlilies* (Paper Swans Press, 2017). He co-edited *Magma* #70 on the theme of 'Europe'. Paul co-curates Poetry in Aldeburgh and lives between Cambridge and Brussels. He interviews poets at 🌐 paulstep.com.   📷 paulstep456   🐦 stephenson_pj

HELEN SULIS BOWIE (they/she) is a writer, performer and charity worker. Their debut pamphlet *WORD/PLAY*, a selection of playable poems, was released by Beir Bua Press in July 2021, and their pamphlet of feminist film trope poetry, *Exposition Ladies*, is due for release with Fly On The Wall Press in Autumn 2022. Helen loves mayonnaise and hates writing third person bios.

TIFFANY ANNE TONDUT has an MA in Poetry from Kingston University. She teaches written and performance poetry for the Women's Centre, Sutton and her work has been commissioned, broadcast and featured in a range of publications. In 2020 she was a winner of the Poetry Archive's Now! Wordview competition. Her debut pamphlet *Wanted* is forthcoming from Broken Sleep Books (2023).

DILA TOPLUSOY is an emerging writer and poet from Istanbul, Turkey. She holds a first class honours degree in Media and Cultural Studies from University of the Arts London. Her work has appeared in several print and online publications including *Sky Island Journal*, *The Pandemic Post*, *Any Segment Magazine* and *The Story Seed*.
🐦 dilaquis   🌐 dilaquis.com

MIKE WEST was born in a hospital and got a 2:1.
🐦 camdenlight

DYLAN WILLOUGHBY is a poet and music producer living in Los Angeles.

◉ lostinstarsmusic

INDEX

Alexander the Great	*42*
Antoinette, Marie	*73*
Aristophanes	*18*
Aristotle	*19*
Armstrong, Neil	*22*
Austen, Jane	*73*
Baudeckinson, Charmily	*37*
Beeton, Isabella	*55*
Bezos, Jeff	*23*
von Bismarck, Otto	*73*
Blake, William	*41*
Bishop Blanckley	*50*
Bowie, David	*49*
Byatt, A. S.	*32*
Caligula	*52*
Camus, Albert	*44*
Captain Pugwash	*58*
Carroll, Lewis	*44*
Churchill, Winston	*16*

Colette	*30*
Columbo	*67*
Dastardly, Dick	*59*
DeVito, Tommy	*35*
Don Corleone	*34*
Don Curlyone	*51*
Drabble, Margaret	*32*
Earhart, Amelia	*28*
Eliot, T. S.	*39*
El Nadi, Lotfia	*29*
Epicurus	*19*
Ferdinand, Franz	*73*
Fletcher, Jessica	*67*
Flintstone, Wilma	*59*
Foucalt, Michel	*70*
Frost, Robert	*80*
Garnet	*59*
Grahame, Kenneth	*33*
Hadrian	*52*
Han Fei	*21*
Heraclitus	*19*

Holmes, Sherlock	*66*
Jackson, Shirley	*63*
Jemison, Mae C.	*23*
Johnson, Amy	*28*
Kahlo, Frida	*45*
Kalep, Elvy	*29*
Katori, Tamaki	*17*
Lamarr, Hedy	*27*
de Laroche, Raymonde	*29*
Lawrence, H. D.	*36*
Lao Tzu	*20*
Leonowens, Anna	*48*
Lispector, Clarice	*24*
Lord Byron	*33*
Machiavelli, Niccolò	*43*
Marcus Aurelius	*53*
Marx, Karl	*77*
Maxwell, Glyn	*39*
McDaniel, Hattie	*61*
McGoohan, Patrick	*72*
McLuhan, Marshall	*25*

Mencius	*21*
de Mille, Agnes	*31*
Miłosz, Czesław	*39*
Miss Marple	*67*
Montana, Tony	*34*
Morgan, Edwin	*68*
Murdoch, Iris	*46-47*
Anaïs Nin	*45*
Pangloss, Peter	*51*
Plutarch	*19*
Pope Alexander VI	*72*
Popeye	*58*
Raffles, A. J.	*57*
Rothstein, Sam 'Ace'	*35*
Sailor Moon	*23*
Sarton, May	*71*
Sartre, Jean-Paul	*33*
S[in]artre, Wallace Frank	*15*
Snoopy	*6*
Socrates	*18*
Spade, Sam	*66*

Sun Tzu	*20*
Tiberius	*53*
Tzara, Tristan	*64*
Vlad the Impaler	*50*
Whistler, Clarence	*54*
Whitson, Peggy	*22*
Williams, William Carlos	*38*
Xun Kuang	*21*
Zelenskyy, Volodymyr	*60*
Zhuangzi (Zhuang Zhou)	*65*

THANK YOU FOR YOUR ATTENTION

THE HIPFLASK SERIES

is an improvised dance of unusual forms and genres, played out across four collaborative, pocket-sized collections. Each book comprises a selection of works that skirt close to (or cross the border into) poetic composition, revealing the dynamic relationship between poetry and other kinds of writing. The major theme of each is extrapolated from one or other of these key aspects of modern poetry – play, appropriation, subtext and conflict – but the result is a series that occupies its own strange niche: mutant miscellanies, oddball assortments. Good for a nip or a slug or a long, deep swig.

SIDEKICK BOOKS

is a London-based small press specialising in collaborative works and experiments in genre.